New ways of photographing the new Masai

the new Masai
are the more
modern masai
living in the
cities

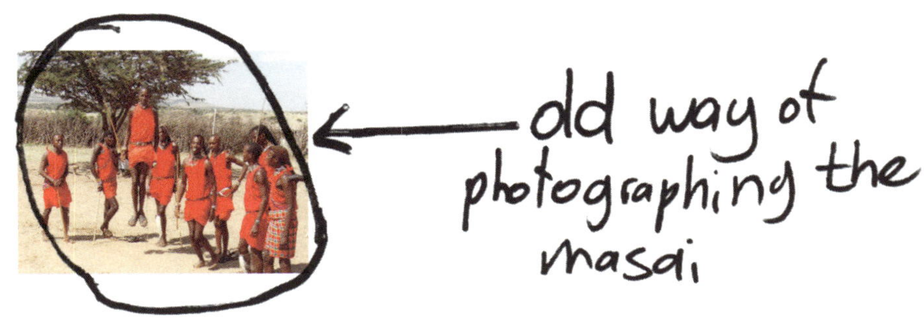

Filémon (30 years)

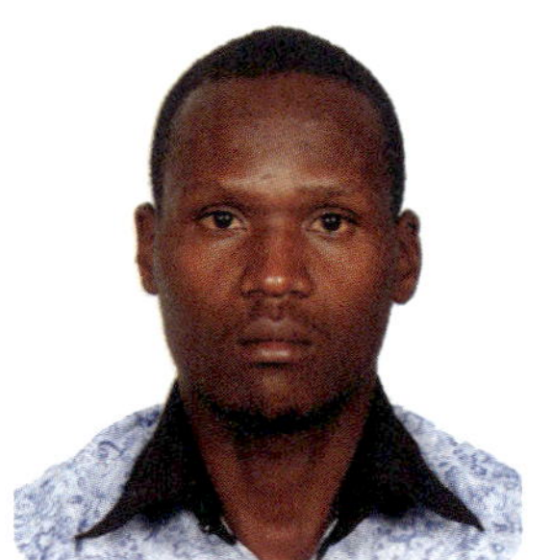

Filémon (30 years)

- Like: To be photographed as a witch doctor

Doesn't like: To be photographed naked

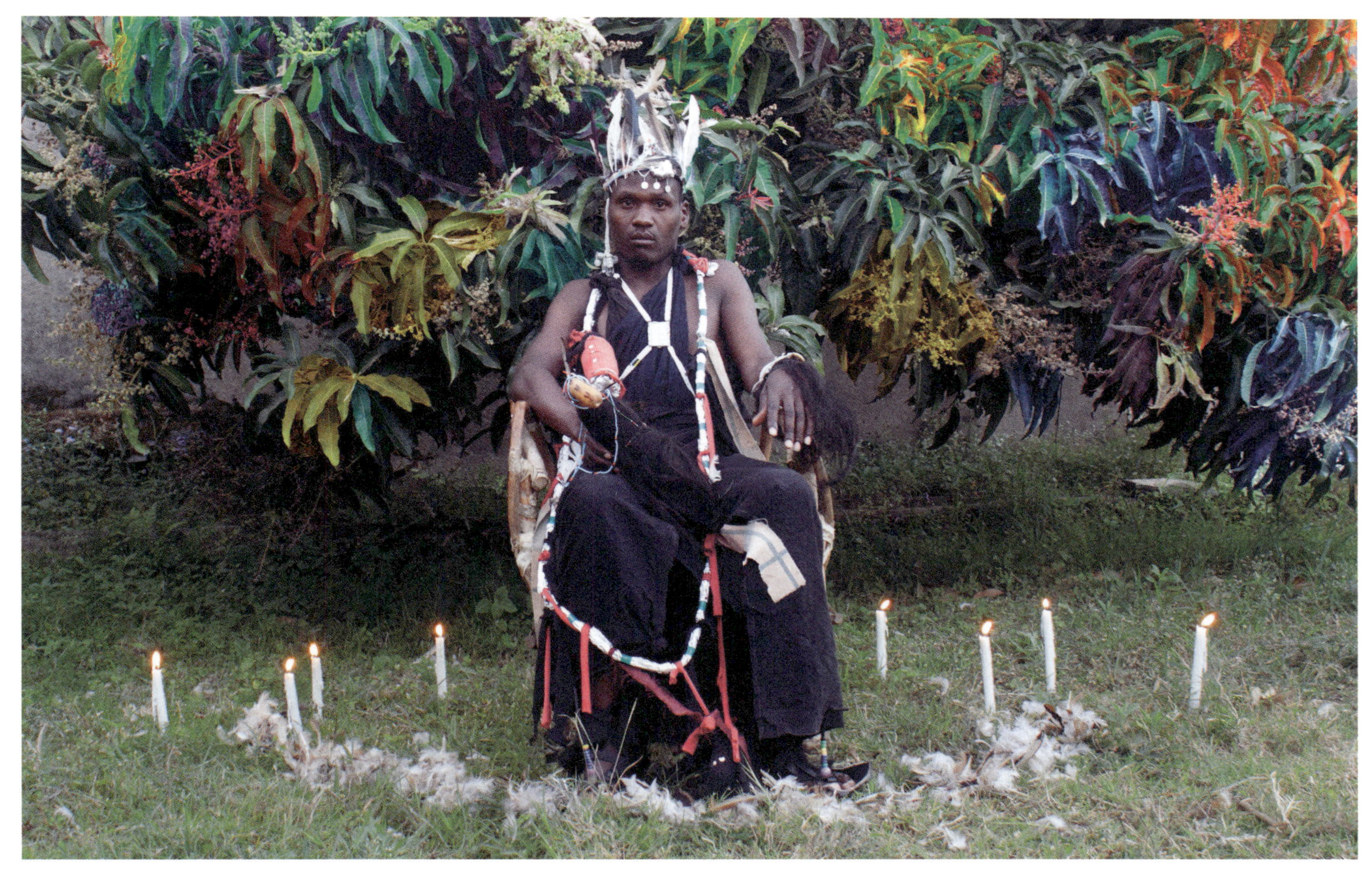

The first choice of Filémon

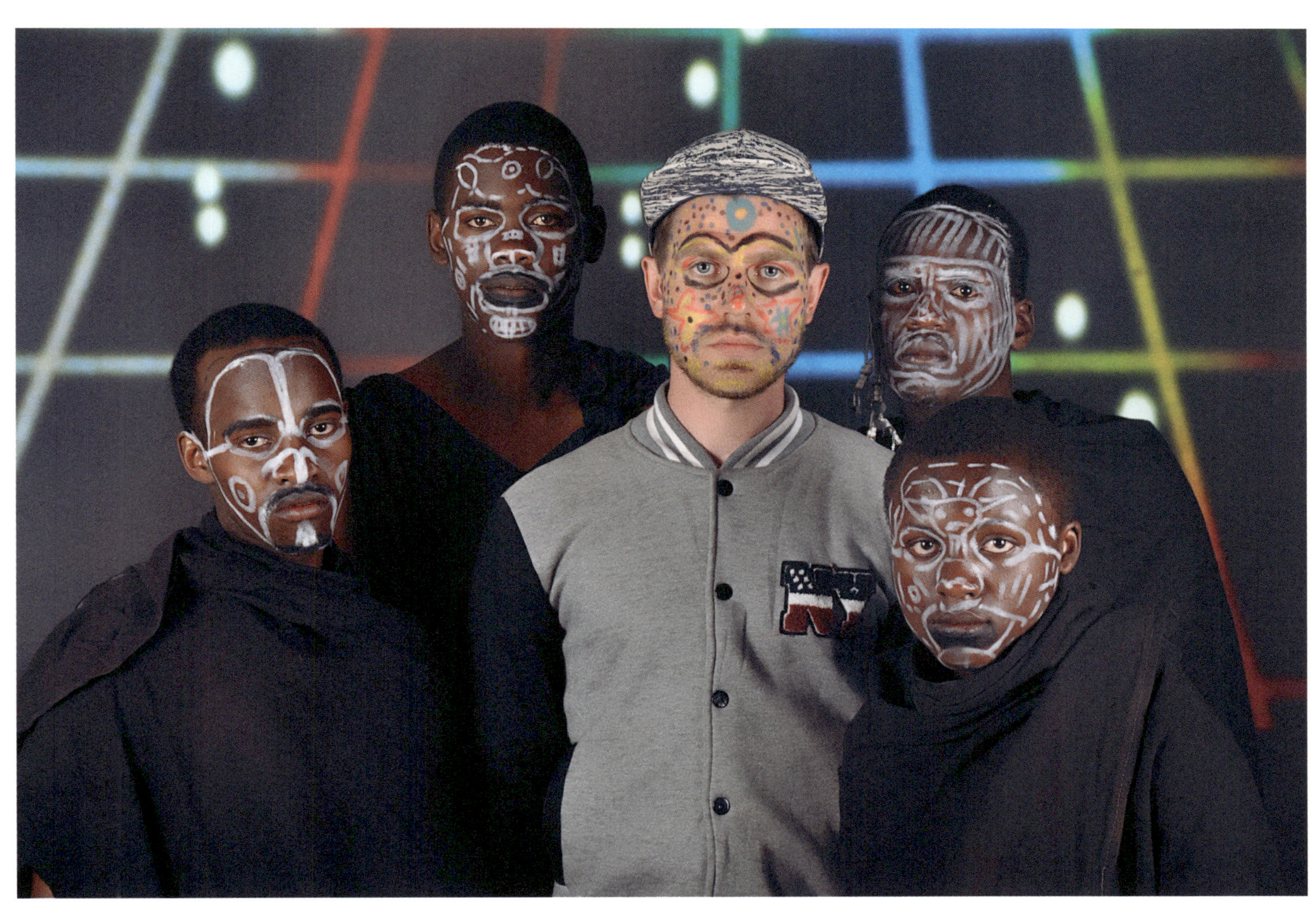

The second choice of Filémon

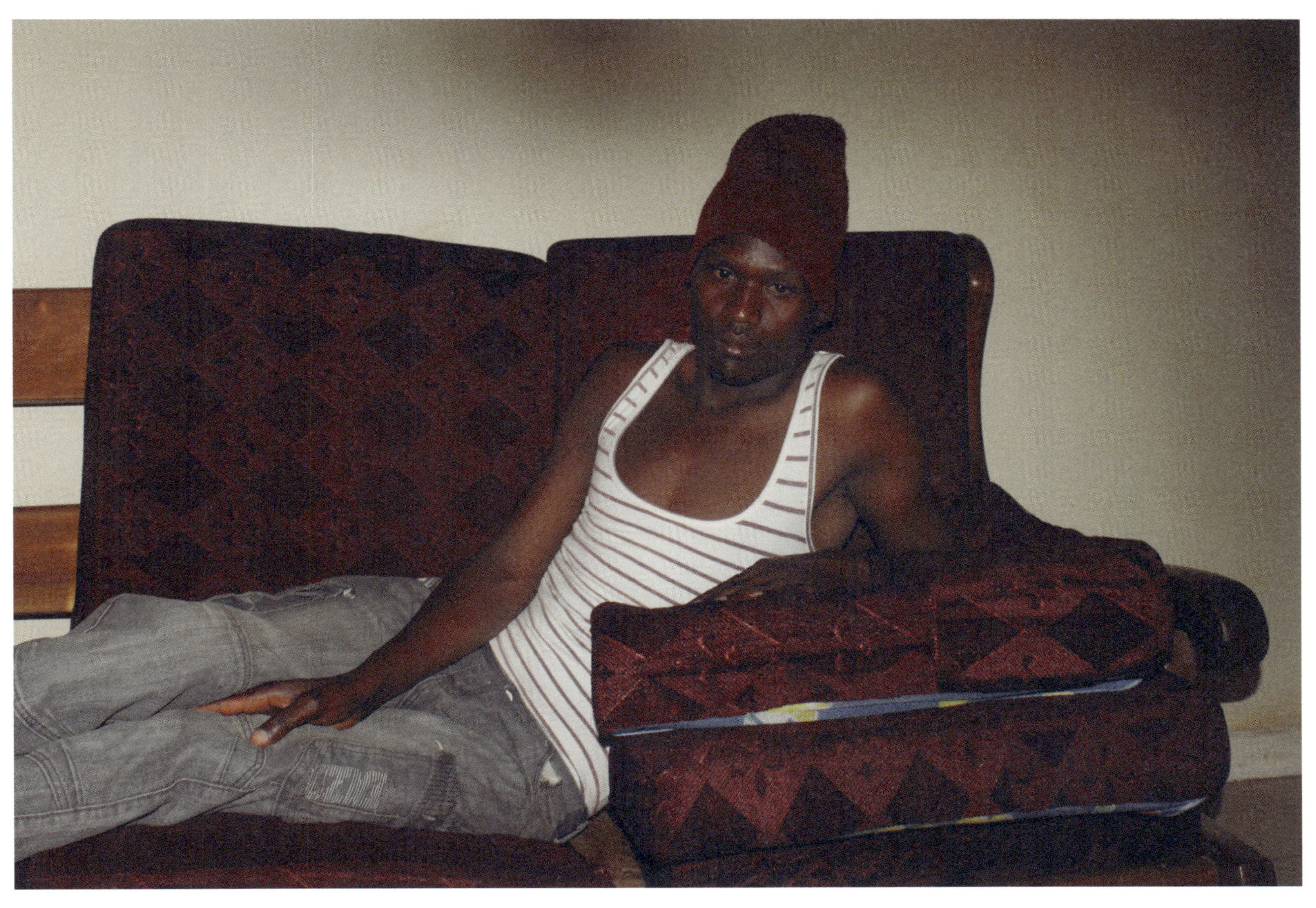

The third choice of Filémon

Secri (27 years)

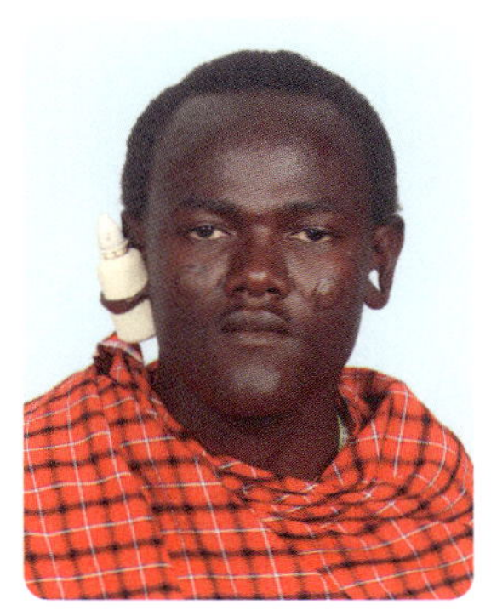

Secri (27 years)

guard

Like: To be photographed just standing, nobody else there

Doesn't like: To be photographed naked

or

with crusty old cars ~~that~~ or other things that stand for low life

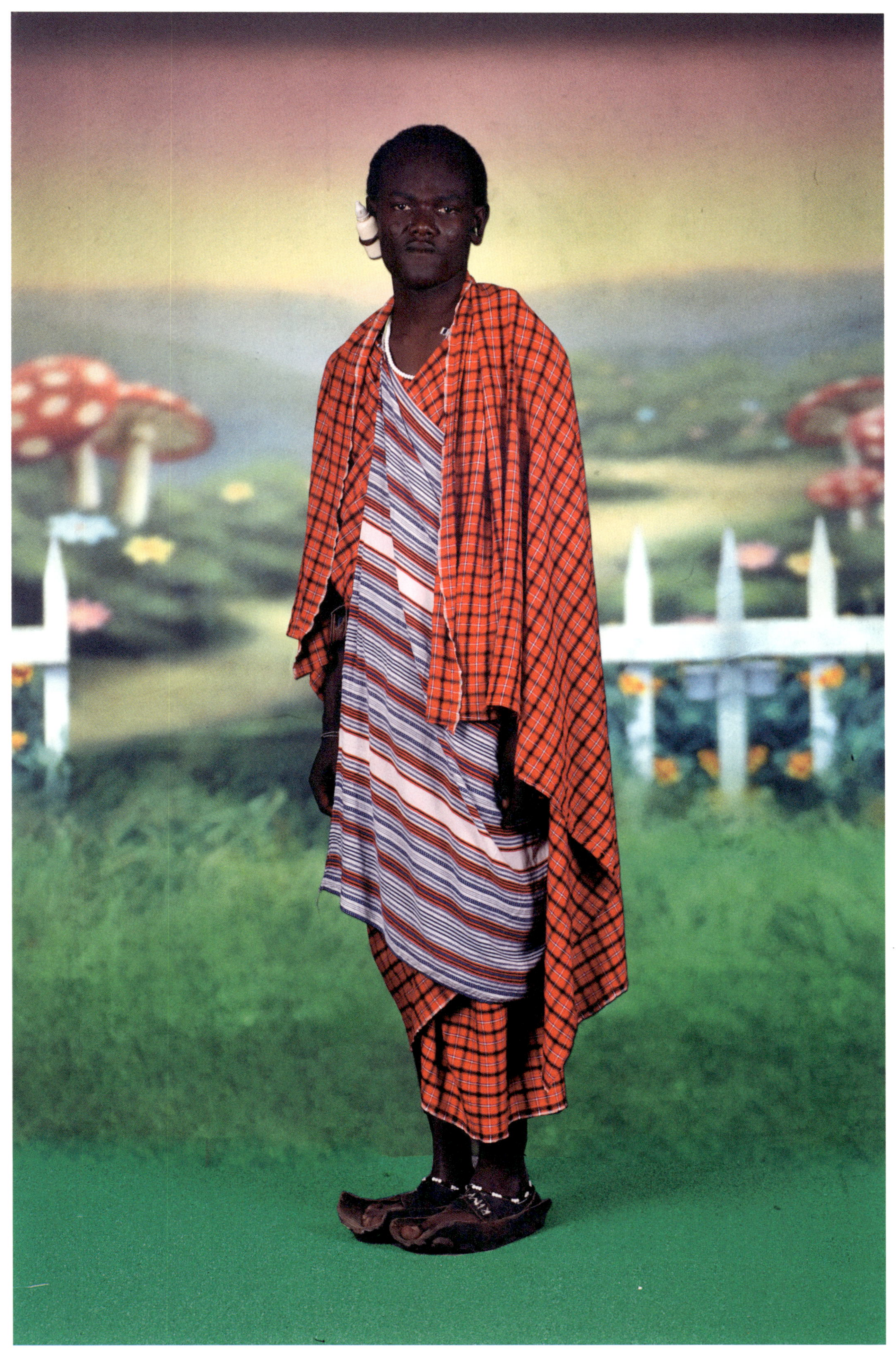

The first choice photo of Seuri

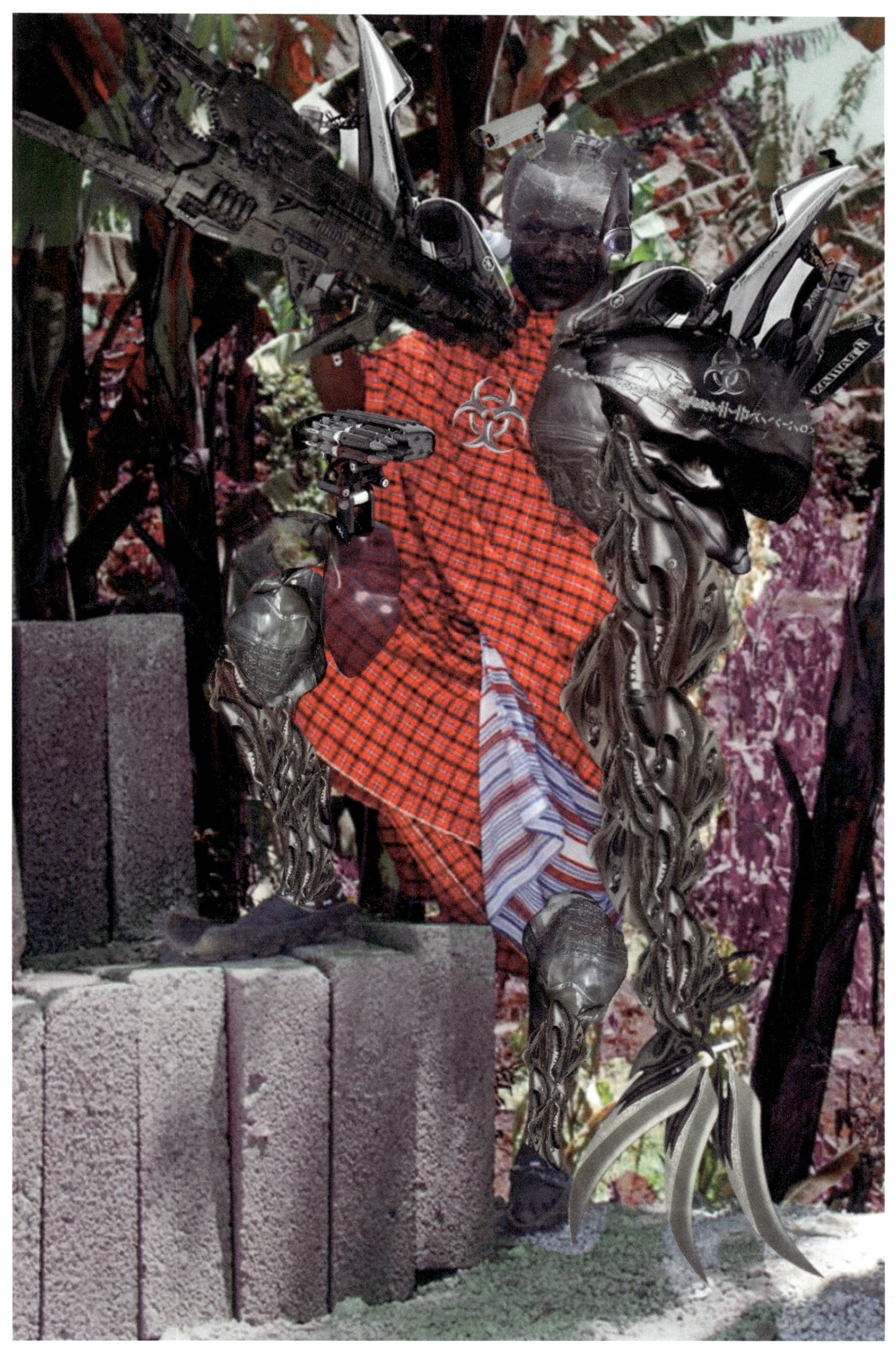

The second choice photo of Secri

in collaboration with Tumblr-star Zimbabwe1992 (London/Zimbabwe)

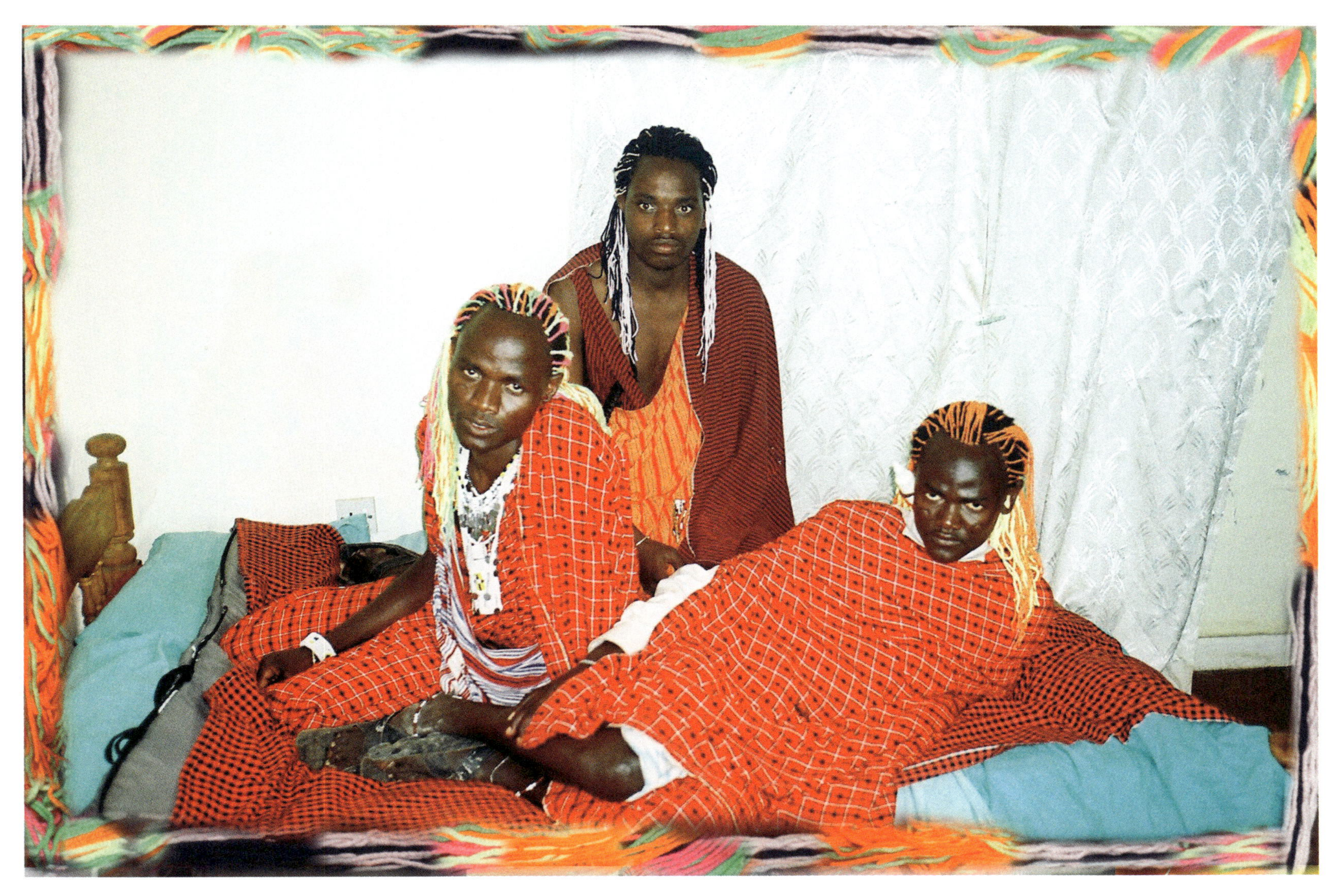

The Third choice photo of Secri

Mike (40 years)

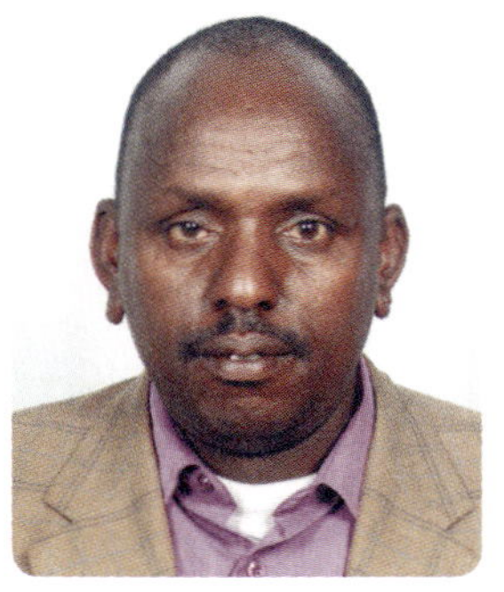

Mike (40 years)

business man

__likes:__ Masais being photographed in a modern way

__Doesn't like:__ Photo's of lazy masai

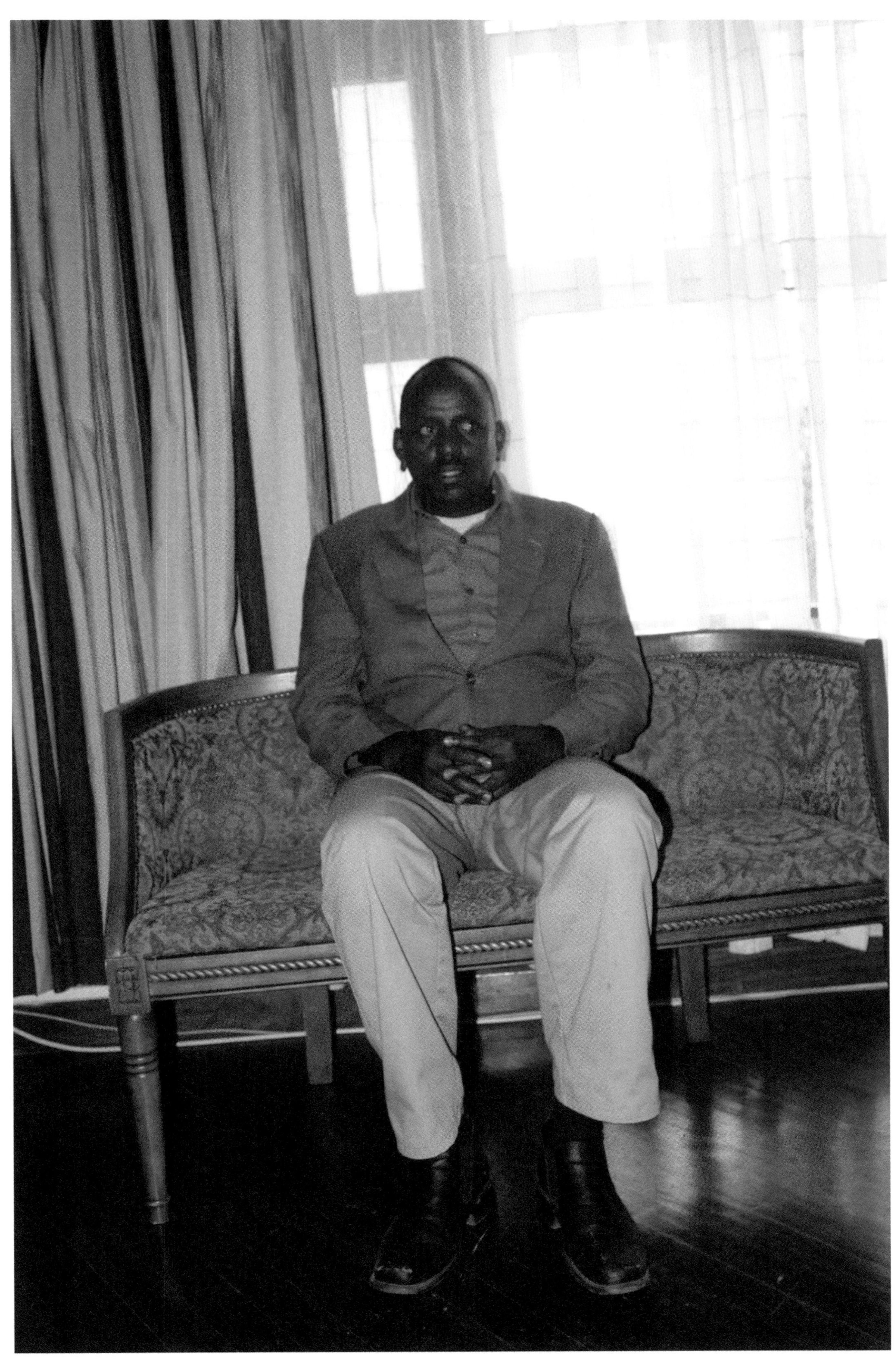

The first choice photo of Mike

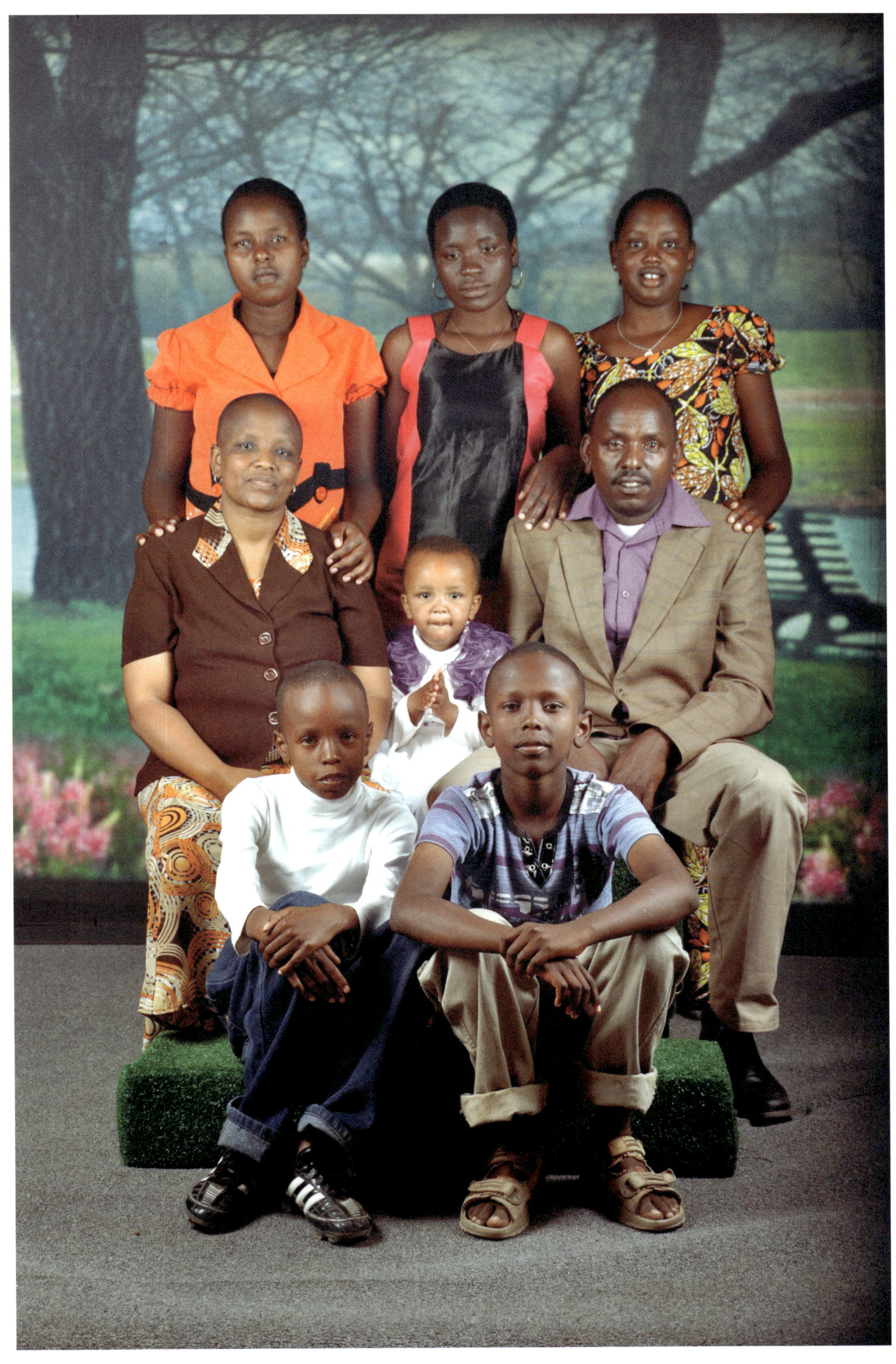

The second choice photo of Mike

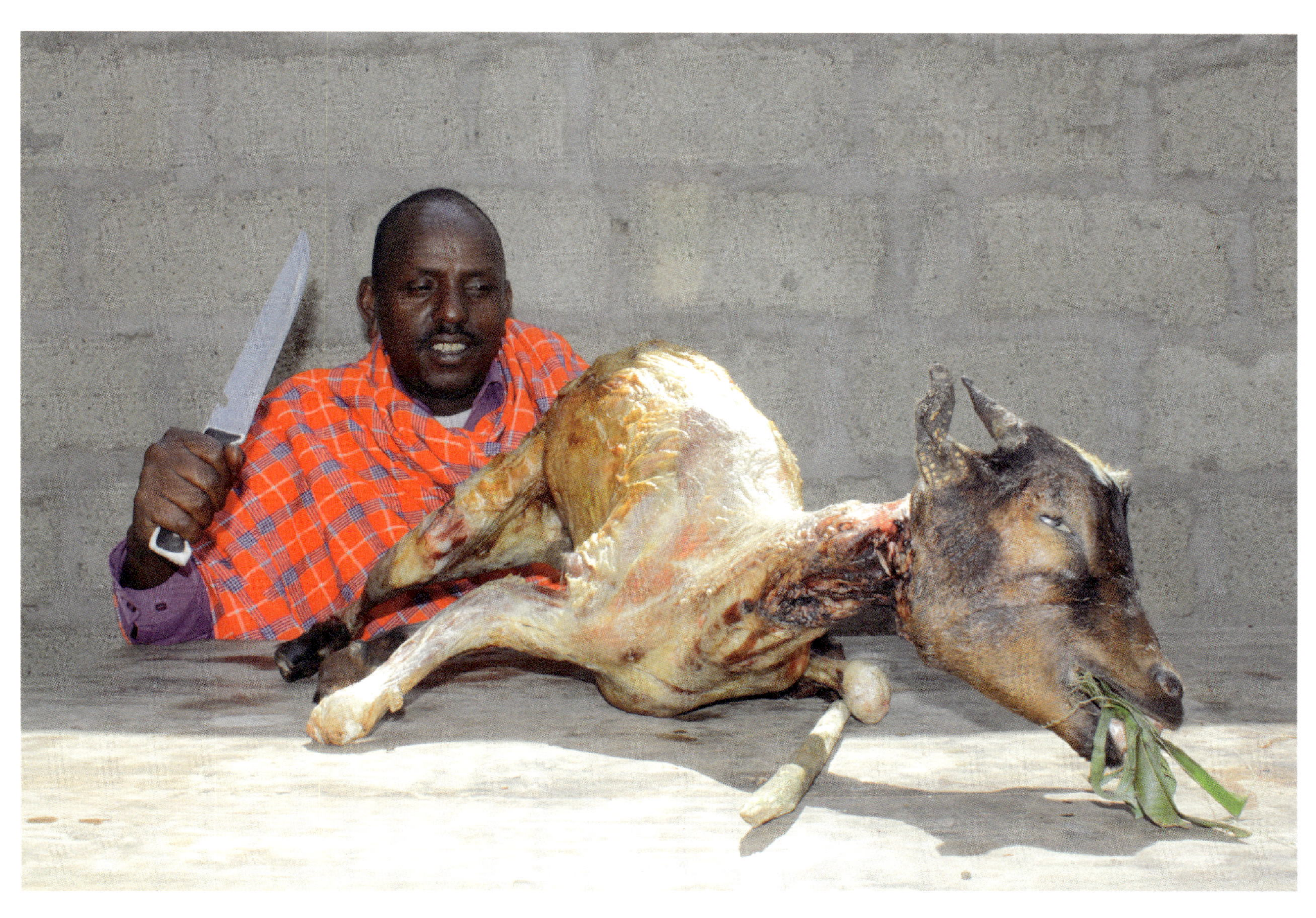

The third choice photo of Mike

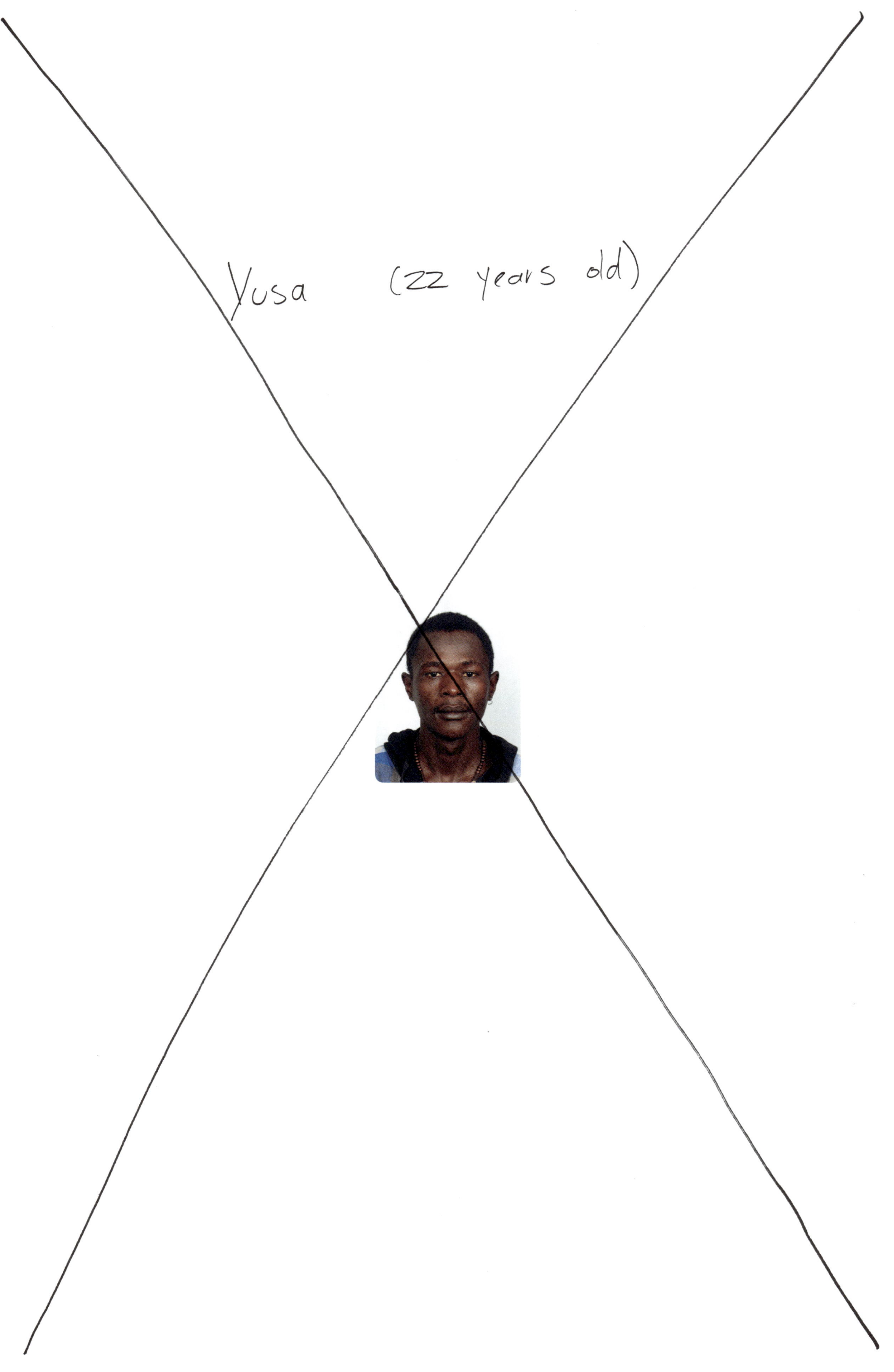
Yusa (22 years old)

Yusa (22 years)

rapper, flycatcher

DISQUALIFIED: LIED ABOUT BEING MASAI

Like: normal photo's

Doesn't like: stupid photo's, like naked photo's

DISQUALIFIED
(not a masai)

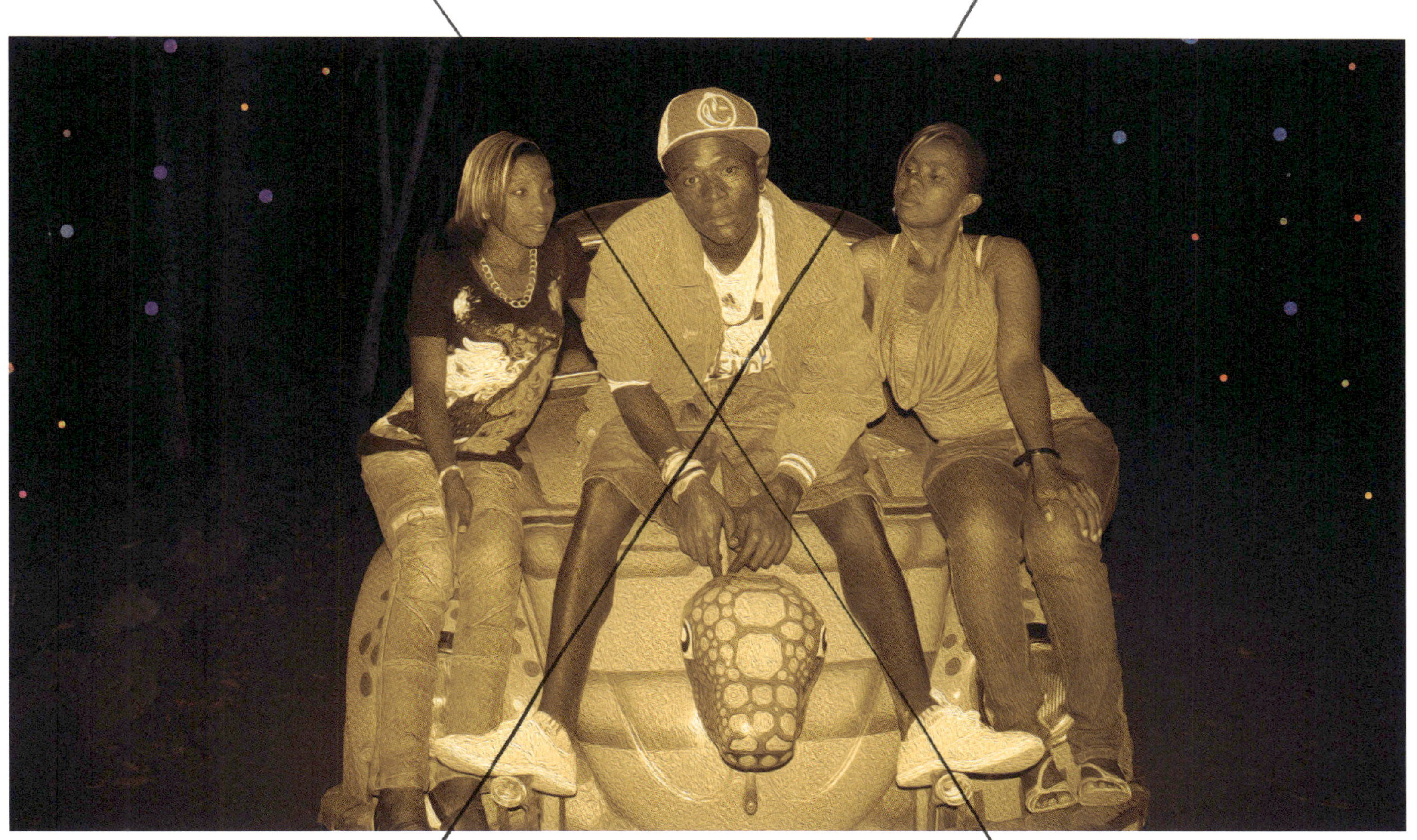

The first choice photo of Yusa

DISQUALIFIED
(not a masai)

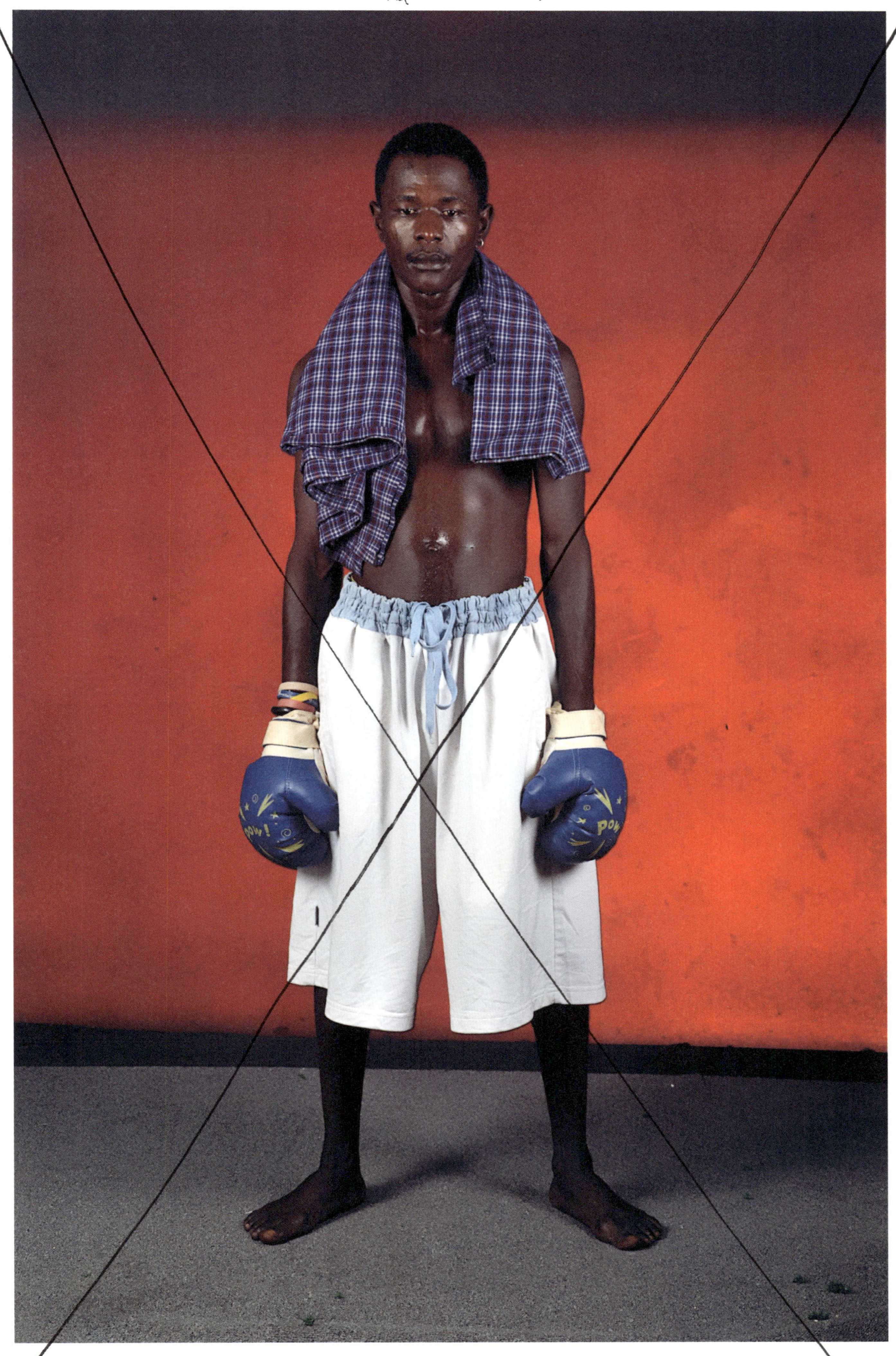

The second choice photo of Yusa

DISQUALIFIED
(not a masai)

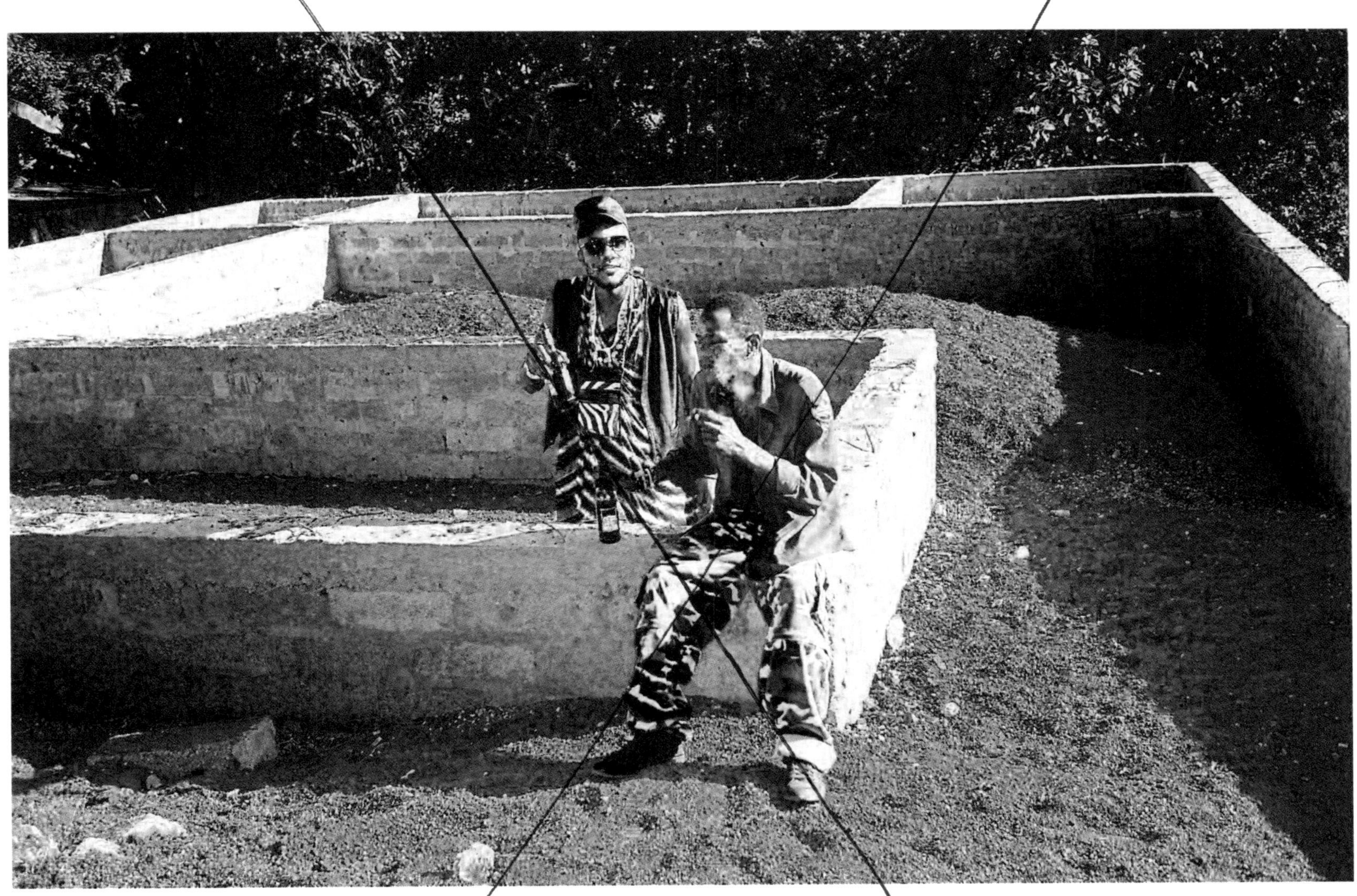

The third choice photo of Yusa

Maria (33 years)

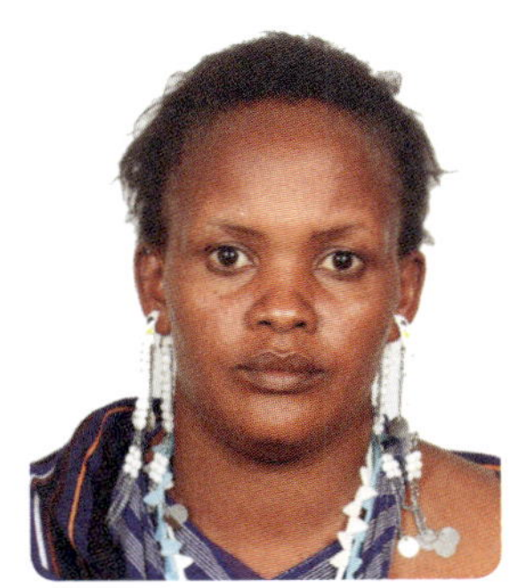

Maria (33 years)

animal keeper

likes: silver and to be photographed happy and smiling

Doesn't like: sad photo's

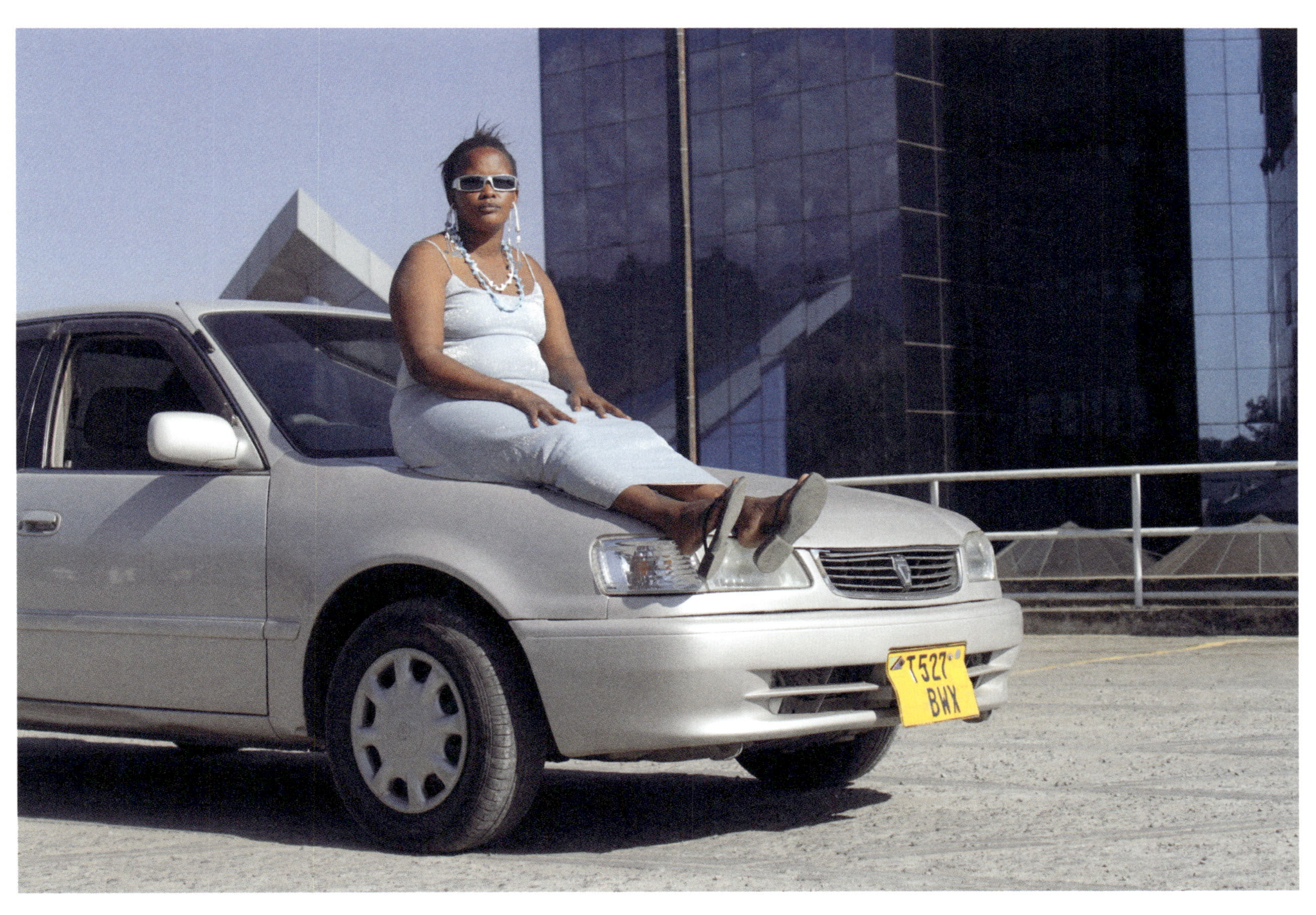

The first choice photo of Maria

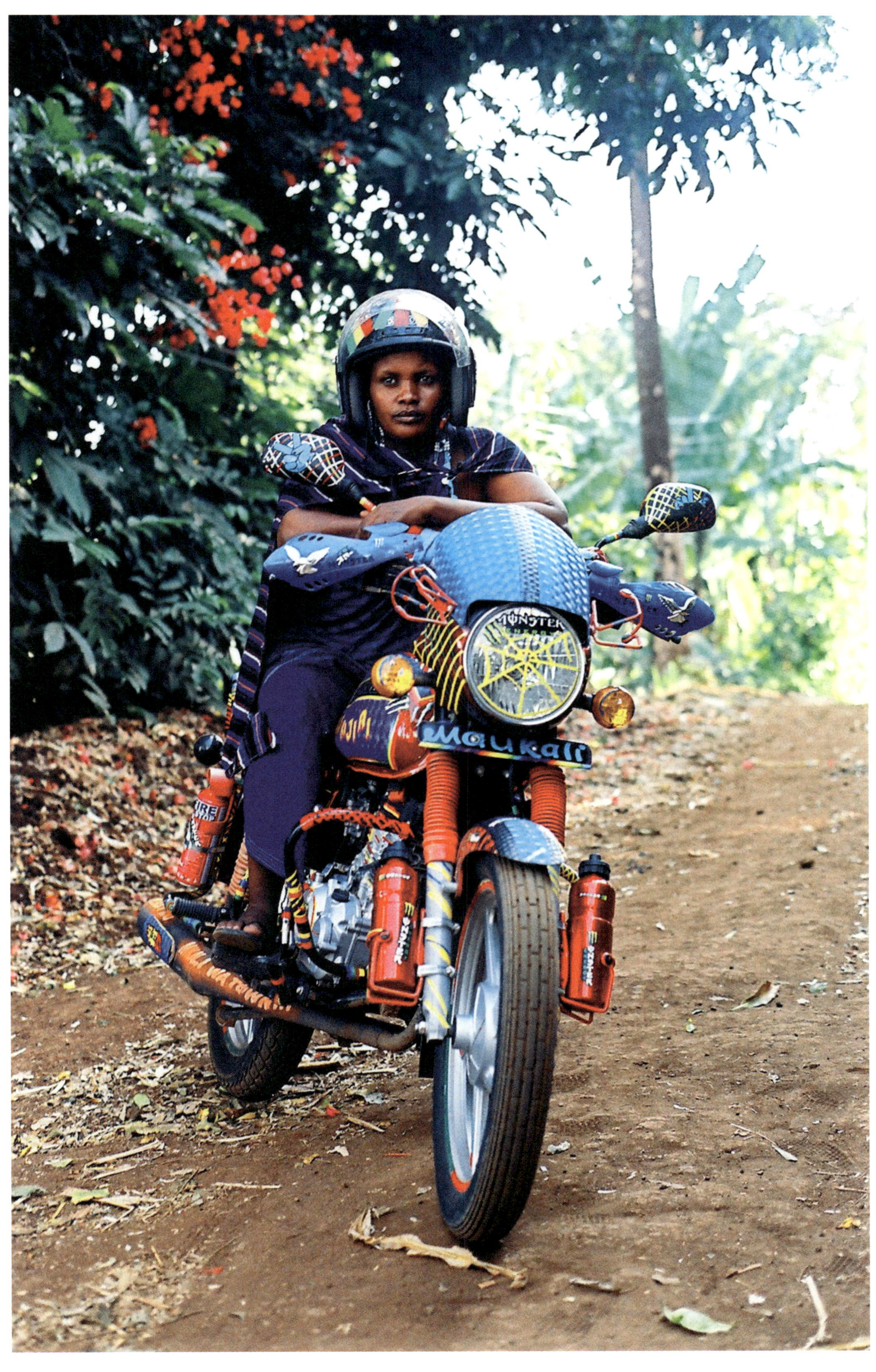

The second choice photo of Maria

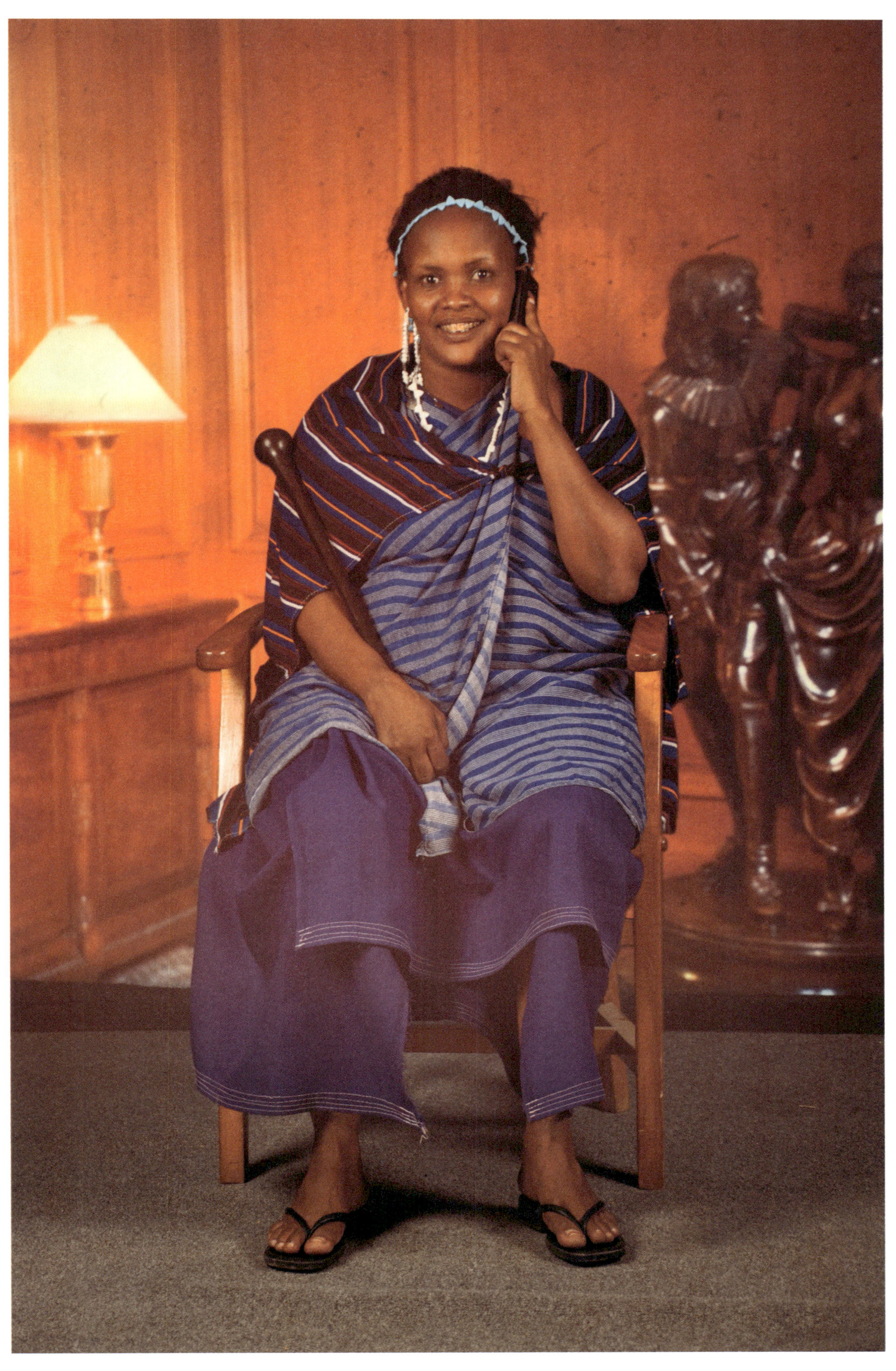

The third choice photo of Maria

Godlisten (23 years)

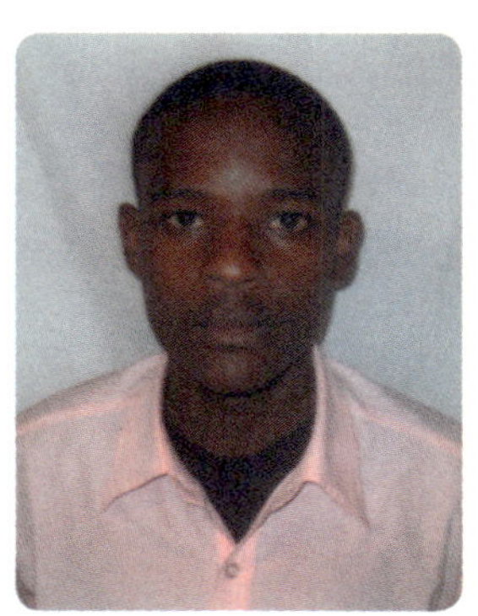

Godlisten (23 years)

film student

like: really colorfull photography and wants to be photographed as a spider

don't like: scary photography

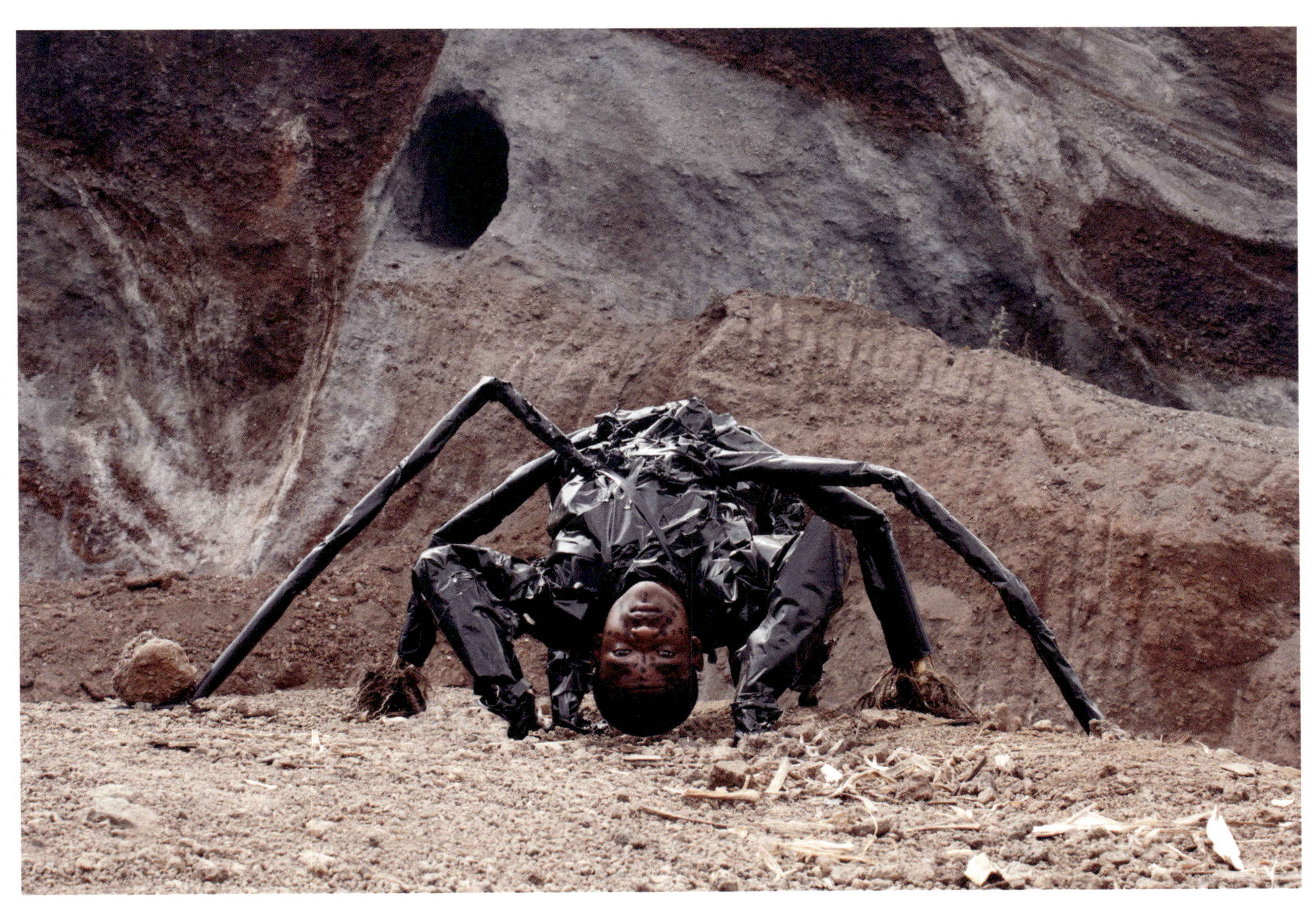

The first choice photo of Godlisten

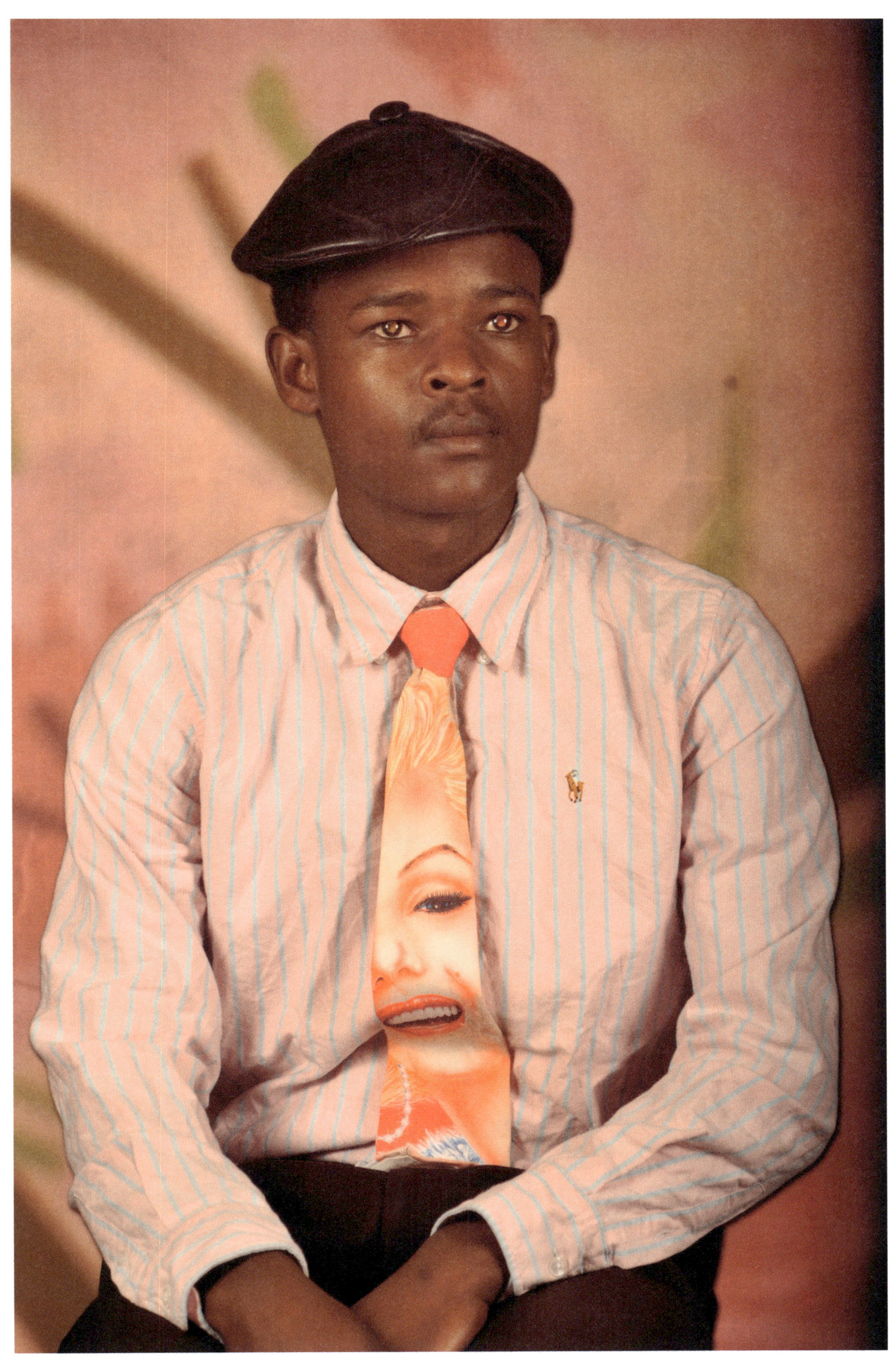

The second choice photo of Godlisten

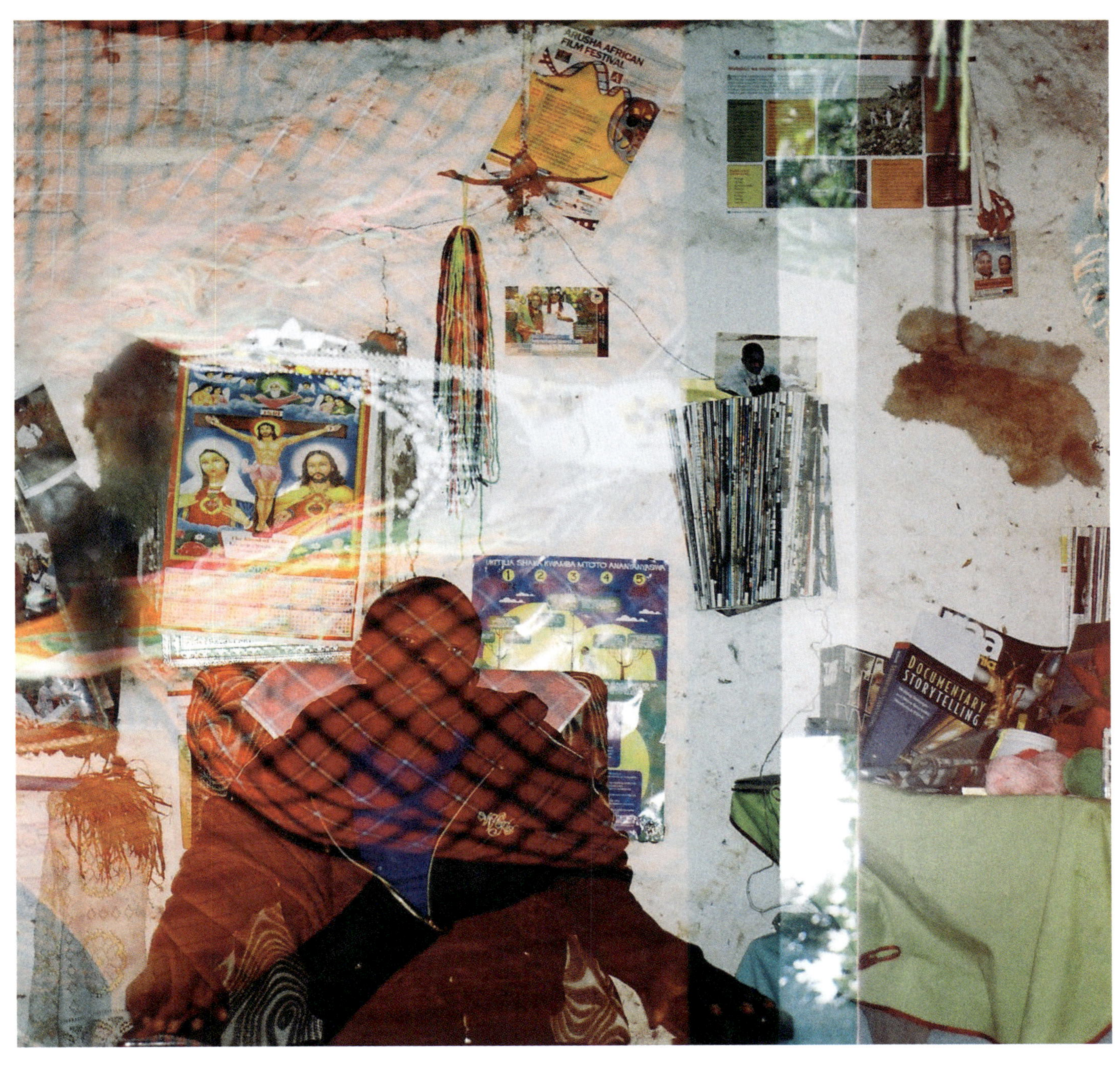

The third choice photo of Godlisten

Eliza (31 years old)

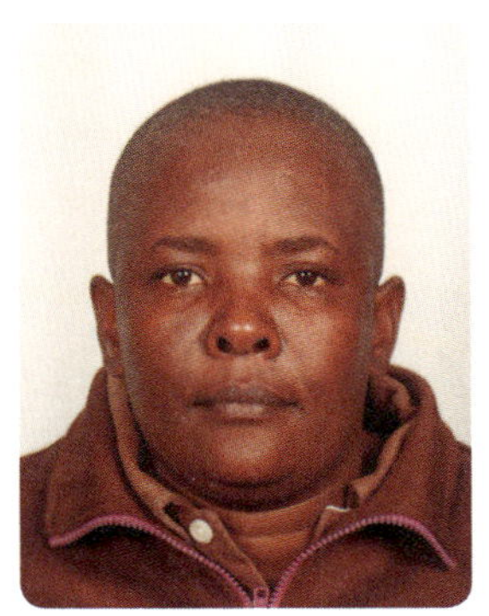

Eliza (31 years old)

(makes little money playing pool in bars against men)

Like: To be photographed really cool, like a gangster girl.

Doesn't like: To be photographed with a lot of make-up or naked

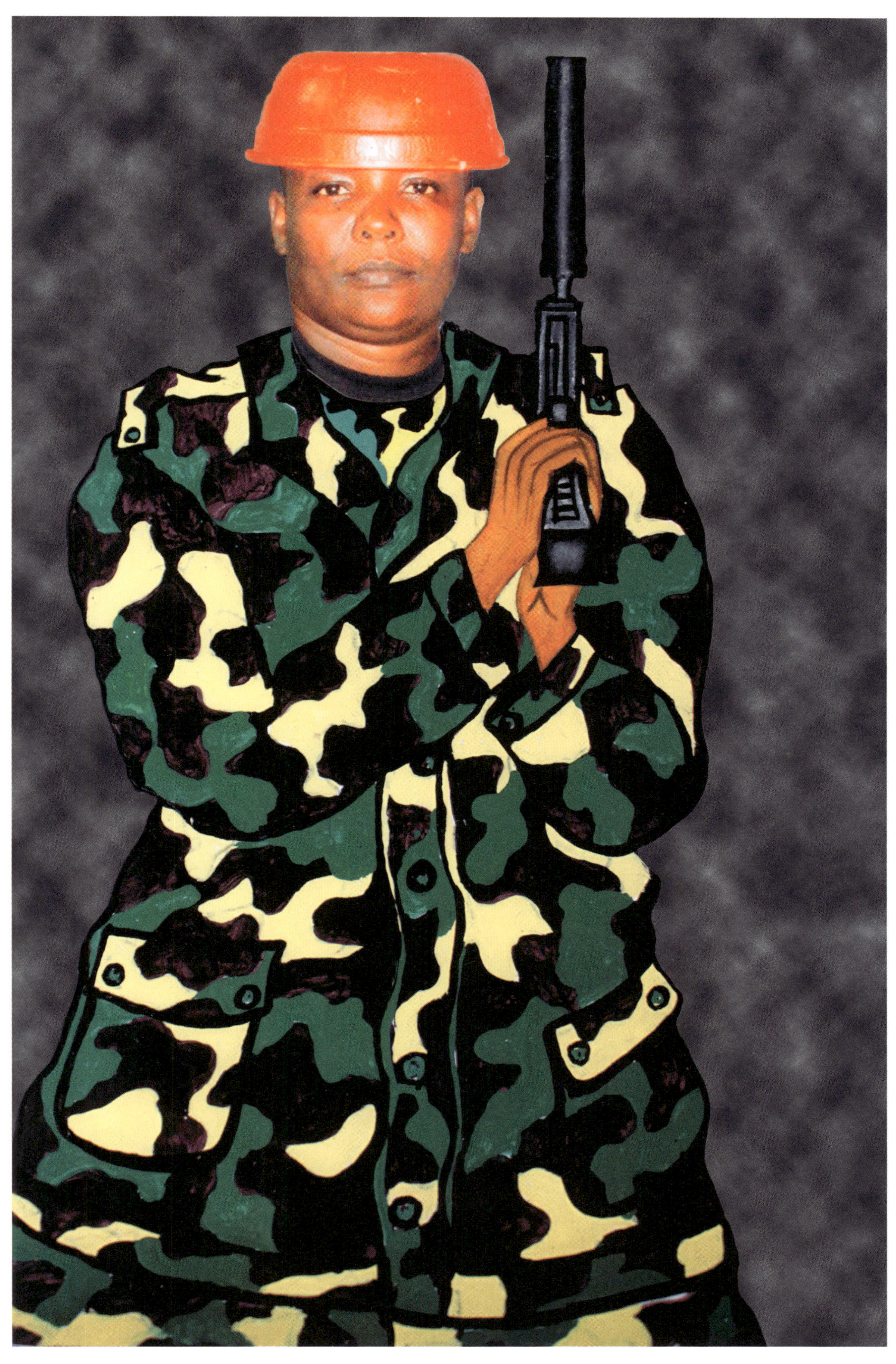

The first choice photo of Eliza

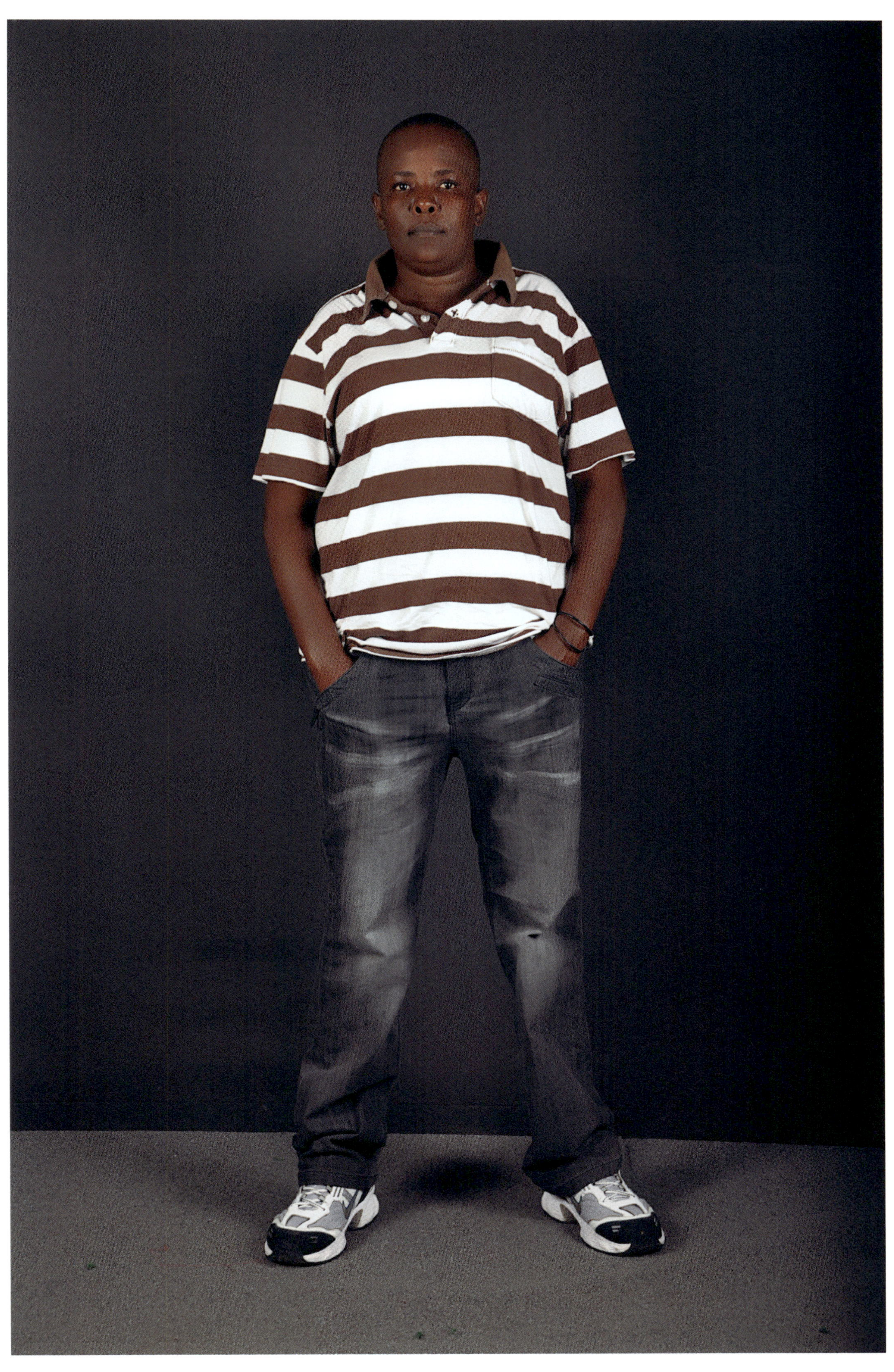

The second choice photo of Eliza

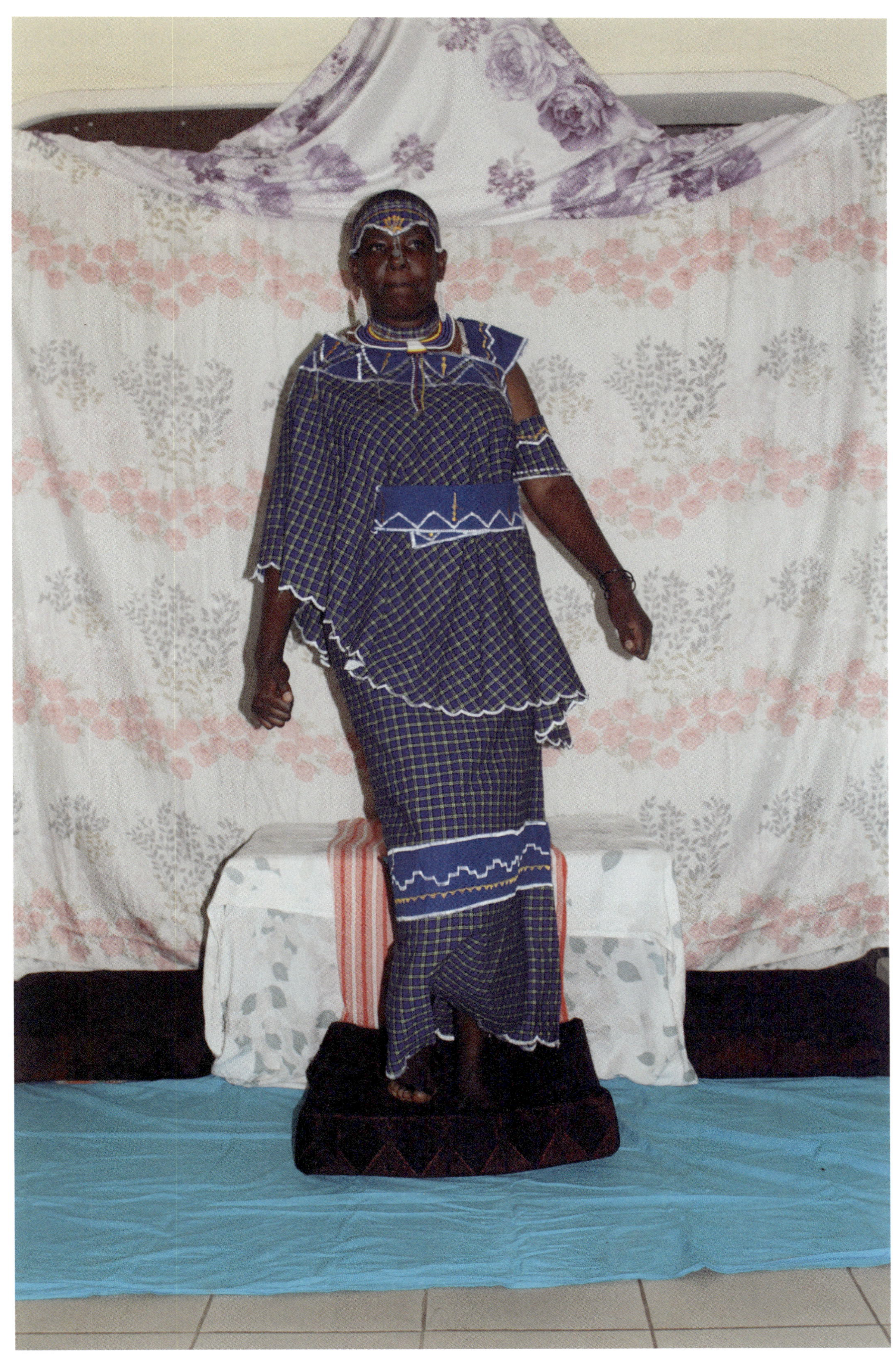

The third choice photo of Eliza

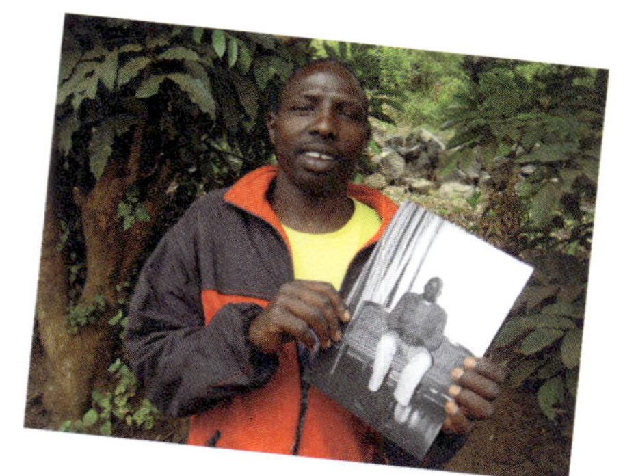

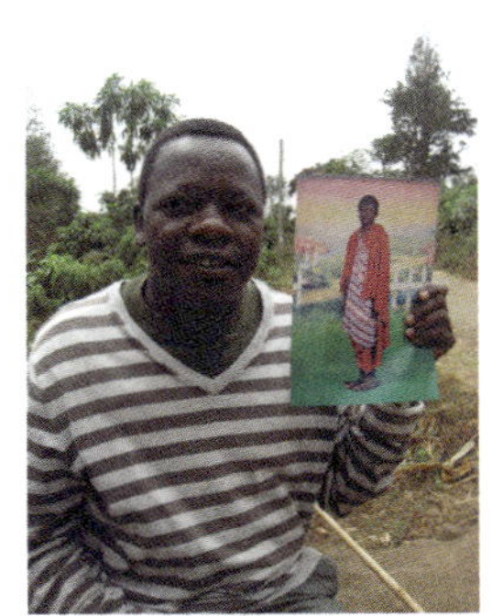

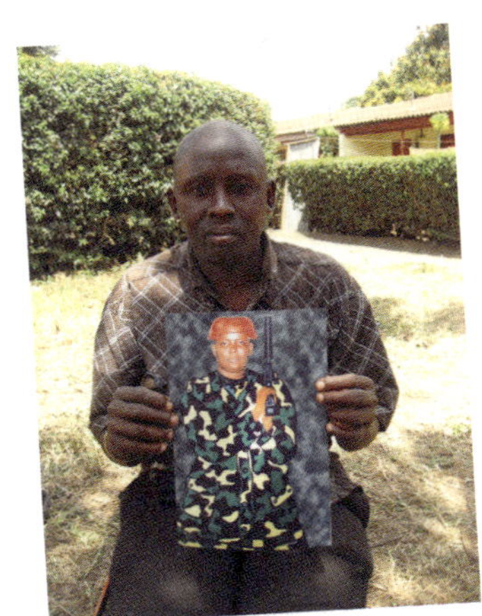

ELECTIONS

50 masais in the city gave their vote

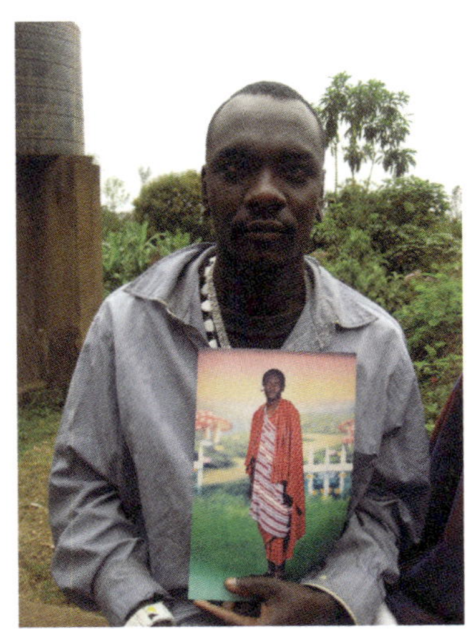

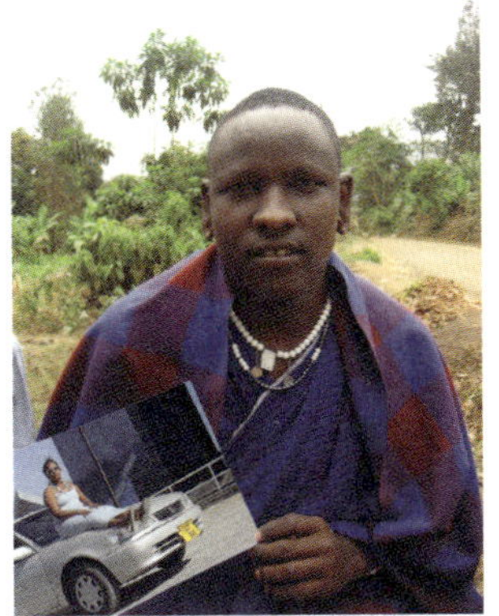

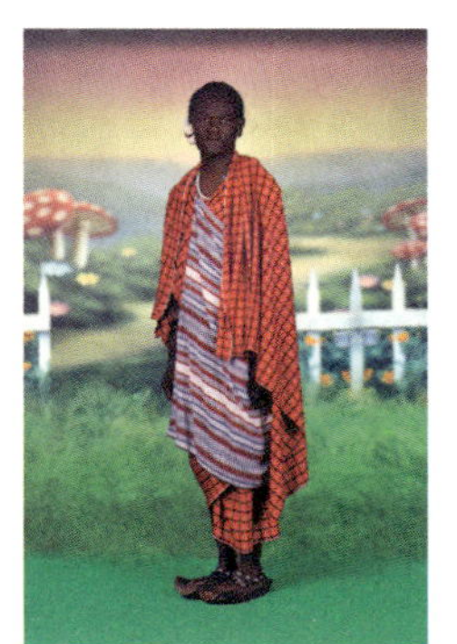

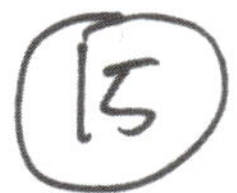

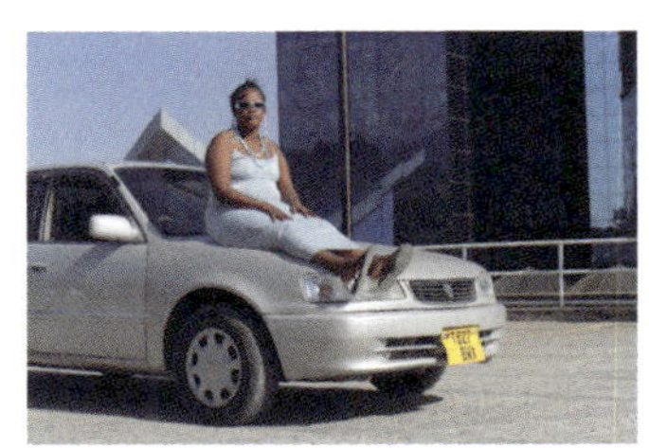

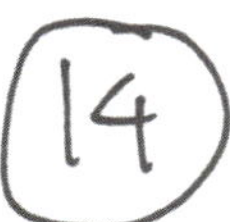

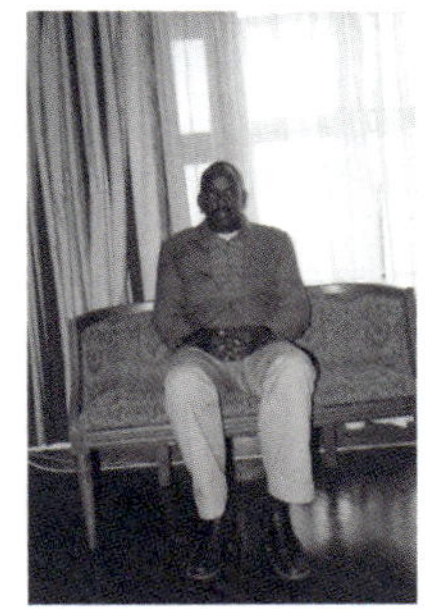

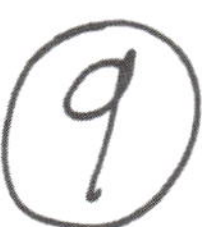

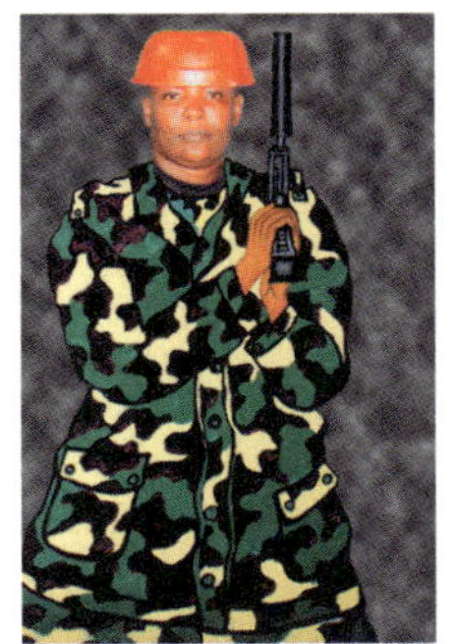

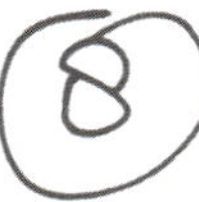

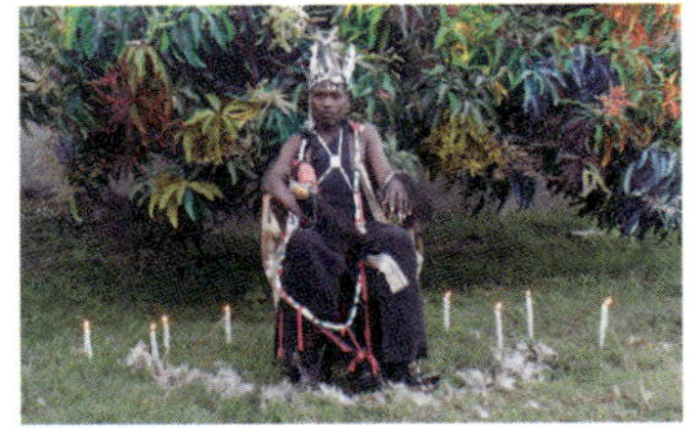

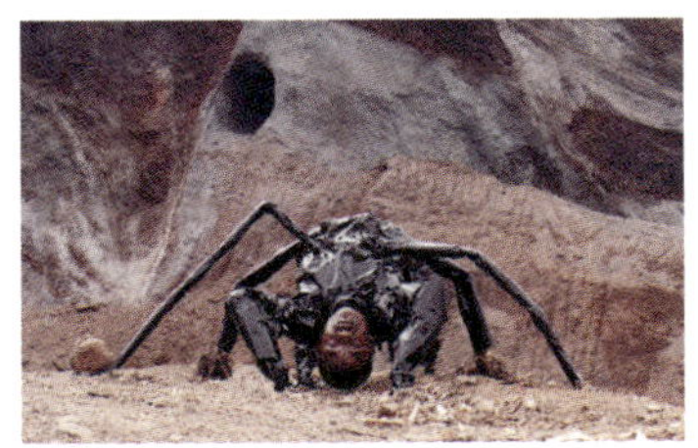

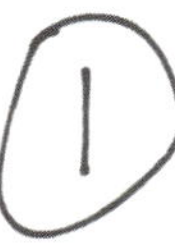

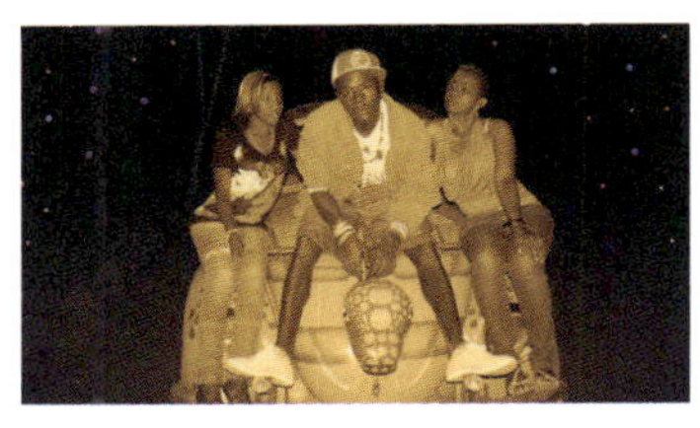

Disqualified

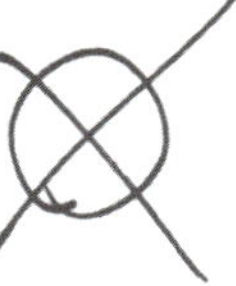

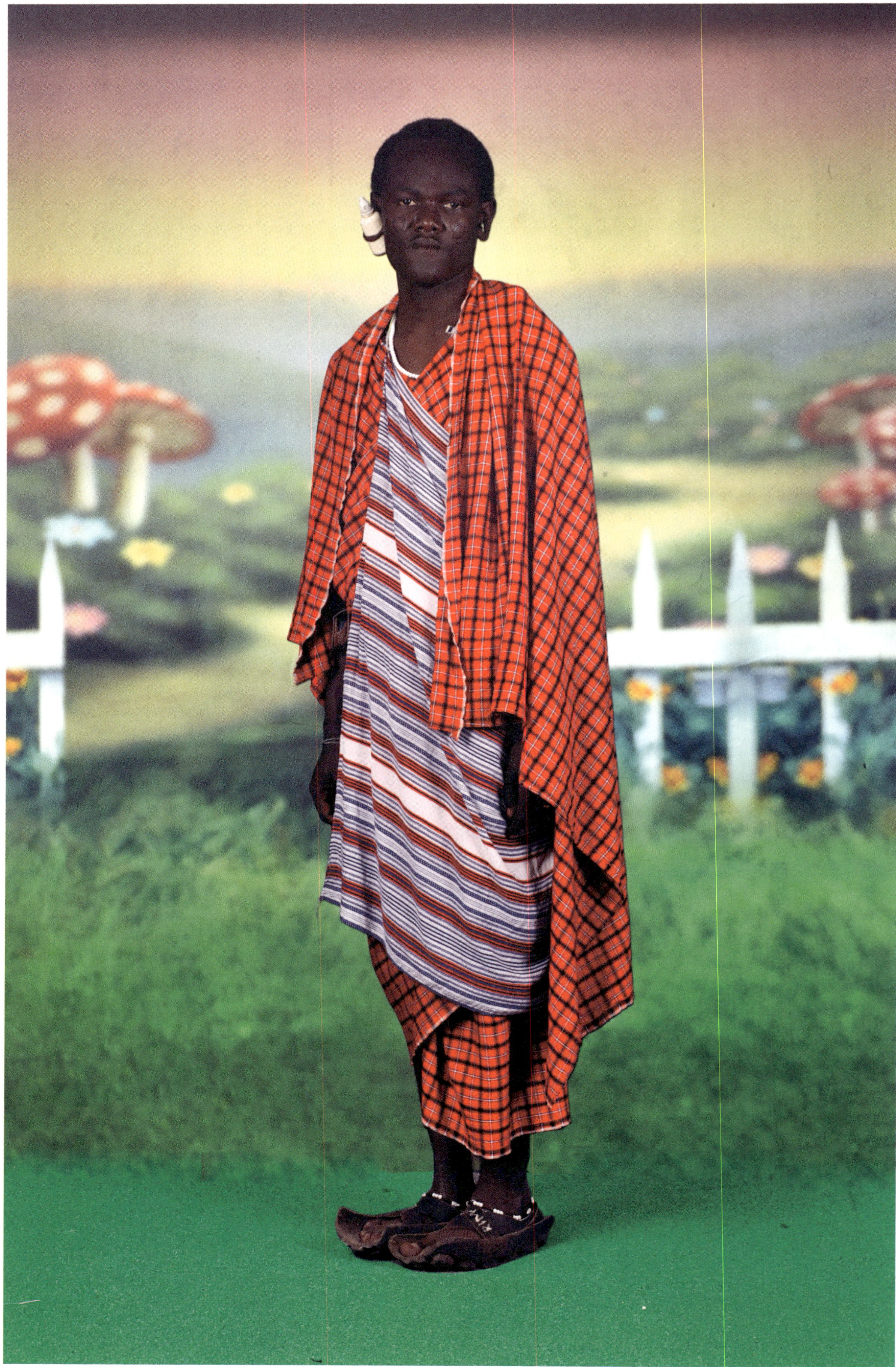